SIMEON
THE SICKLE CELL
HERO

Copyrights

Acknowledgment

We would like to express our deepest gratitude to everyone who helped bring Simeon the Sickle Cell Hero to life and to those who were an important part of Simeon's journey.

To our beloved son, Simeon — your courage, kindness, and light inspire us every single day. You are the heart of this book, and through its pages, your legacy lives on.

To Simeon's siblings, Tj & Gigi— thank you for loving your brother so deeply and for continuing to share his joy with the world. You are heroes in your own way.

To Dr. Corey Hebert — thank you for your medical expertise, insight, and dedication to helping families understand and navigate sickle cell disease. Your guidance has made this story both accurate and impactful.

To Simeon's wonderful teachers — Mr. Brown, Ms. Harris, Ms. Rue, and Mrs. Franklin — thank you for believing in him, encouraging his dreams, and pouring so much love into his education. Your influence shaped his confidence and creativity.

To Mary McLeod Bethune Elementary Charter School in New Orleans, Louisiana — Ms. Smith (Principal) and Mrs. Watson (Assistant Principal) — and the entire faculty and staff, thank you for creating a nurturing, encouraging environment where Simeon could learn, grow, and shine.

To Joshua, our project manager with Elite Studio — thank you for guiding this book from idea to reality, and for believing in the importance of Simeon's story.

To the talented illustrators at Elite Studio — your creativity and skill brought Simeon's world to life in the most beautiful way. We are forever grateful for your work.

To our family, friends, and community — your love, prayers, and unwavering support have carried us through this journey.

Finally, to every child and family living with sickle cell disease — this book is for you. You are strong. You are seen. You are heroes.

About the Authors

Tremaine & Cierra Thompson are devoted parents and a loving married couple from New Orleans, Louisiana. Inspired by their son Simeon's courage and joy, they created Simeon the Sickle Cell Hero to share his story with the world.

Simeon always dreamed of becoming both an author and a doctor. Though he is no longer here to complete that mission, Tremaine and Cierra are carrying his dreams forward, honoring his legacy, and inspiring other children to believe in their own strength and possibilities. In addition to writing, they are dedicated community advocates and founders of a children's wellness brand, working to educate, empower, and support families affected by health challenges.

In loving memory of Simeon Thompson.
For every child who turns pain into power
and every dreamer with a mission.

Once Upon a Time...
There lived a little boy named Simeon,
who had the brightest smile, the biggest heart,
and a magical bracelet that shimmered
when someone was in pain.

One night, the stars danced louder than usual. Simeon's bracelet began to glow, and the wind whispered, It's time.

His bed turned into a flying cloud.
His blanket became a shimmering cape.
He looked down and whispered,
"Let's help someone tonight."

Whenever a child cried out in pain from sickle cell, Simeon's bracelet blinked like a shooting star.

That was his sign—it was go time!

Suddenly, purple bubbles popped all around! Mrs. Franklin's laughter came with them. She sent Simeon ticklish riddles to remind him

"Healing starts with joy."

A beam of sunlight poured from the clouds.
Ms. Harris gentle voice echoed:
"Drink water. Rest. And remember
your light makes things grow."

Back at home, Gigi was stirring smoothie juice.
TJ powered up the Hero Van with his dance moves.
"Call us if you need backup!" they shouted.

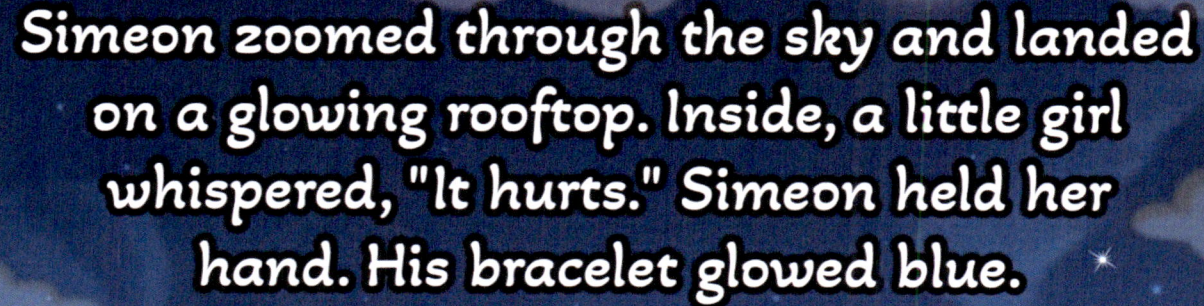

Simeon zoomed through the sky and landed on a glowing rooftop. Inside, a little girl whispered, "It hurts." Simeon held her hand. His bracelet glowed blue.

Out came a giggle patch, a bottle of "Hope Cells,"
a fruit snack called "Bravery Bites,"
and a tiny song that wrapped around the room like a hug.

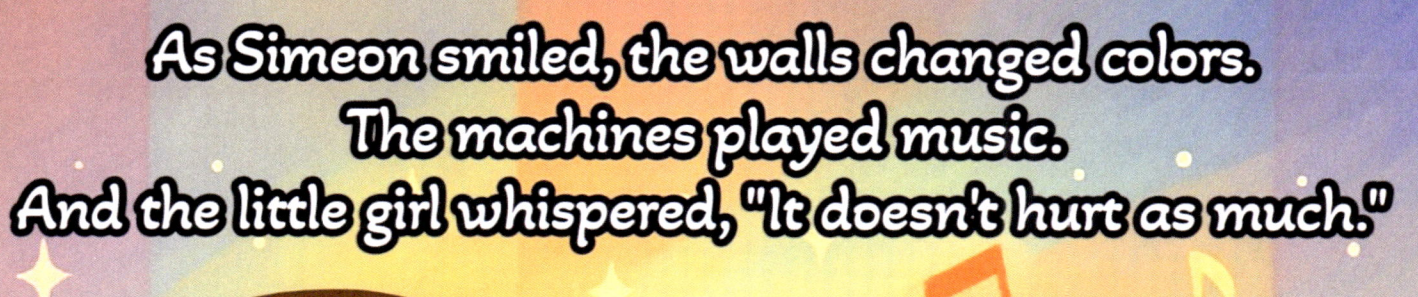

As Simeon smiled, the walls changed colors.
The machines played music.
And the little girl whispered, "It doesn't hurt as much."

Each time Simeon flew off, he left a tiny sticker

You matter.

It glowed whenever someone believed in themselves.

From New Orleans to Jamaica, to a sky palace above Middle East, Simeon visited clouds and castles, whispering healing songs.

Ms. Rue brought purple and blue socks.
Mr. Brown told a story from the stars.
Mrs. Franklin sang a silly song.
Ms. Harris brought warm tea in a floating cup.

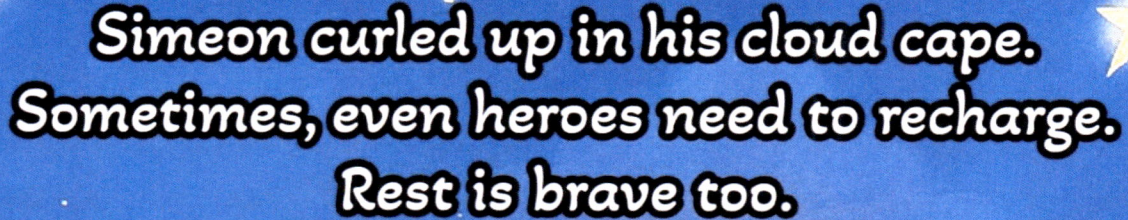

Simeon curled up in his cloud cape.
Sometimes, even heroes need to recharge.
Rest is brave too.

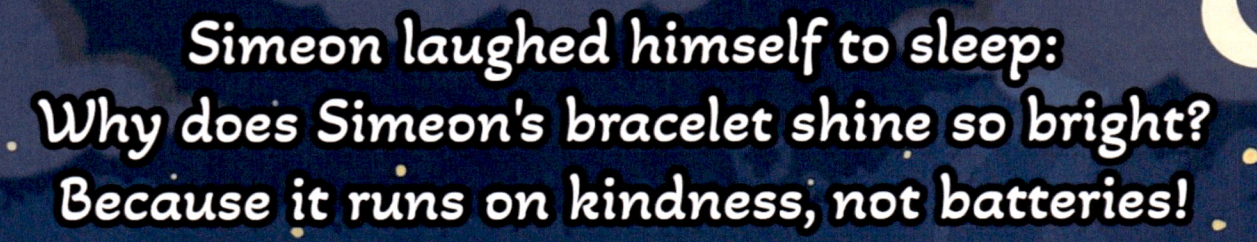

Simeon laughed himself to sleep:
Why does Simeon's bracelet shine so bright?
Because it runs on kindness, not batteries!

He dreamed of writing books, helping kids,
and turning every hospital into a healing room.

Back home, his family tucked his story in their hearts.
His light lives in every hug, every tear, every smile.

Every time you speak up, share a hug, or care for someone hurting you become part of Simeon's story.

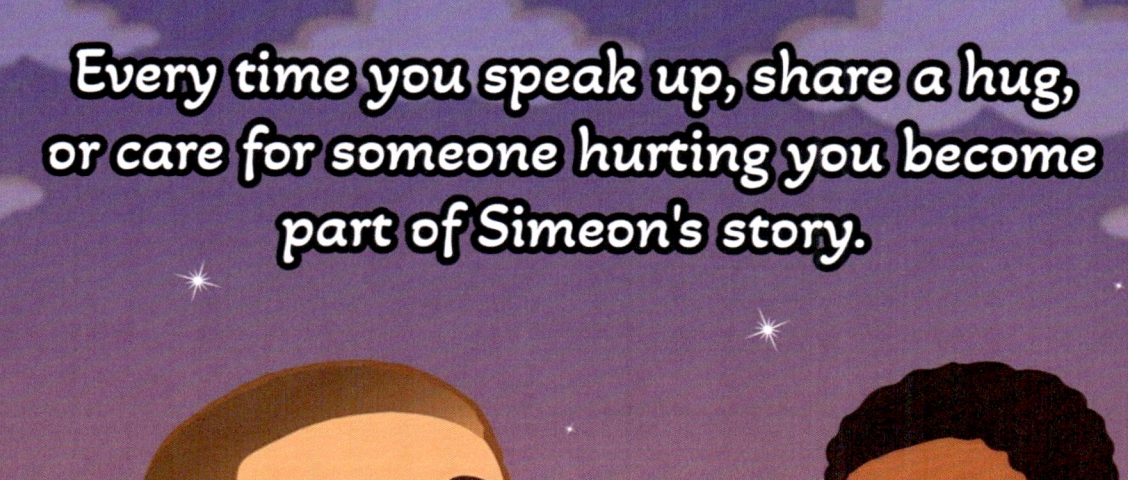

Dr. Corey Hebert, M.D.

As a physician, my mission is to heal but sometimes, my patients bring healing to me. Simeon was one of those patients. He lived with sickle cell disease, a condition that affects over 100,000 people in the United States and occurs in 1 out of every 363 African American births. This disease causes red blood cells to become misshapen, making it difficult for oxygen to travel efficiently through the body. The result can be unpredictable and intense pain episodes, known as "crises," that can disrupt every aspect of life. Through Simeon, I was reminded that while medicine is important, so is the power of the human spirit. Decreasing stress, eating well, and choosing to live the best life possible isn't just good advice it's truly the best medicine.

There is no cure but prevention, treatment, education, and early intervention can save lives.

Awareness like what you're reading right now is where change begins.

www.ingramcontent.com/pod-product-compliance
Lightning Source LLC
Chambersburg PA
CBRC090830120626
46547CB00008B/649